KIDSTUFF
with Willie

ITV BOOKS

Published by

Independent Television Books Ltd
247 Tottenham Court Road
London W1P 0AU

In association with Michael Joseph Ltd

First published 1982
© Roger Goffe, 1982

ISBN 0 900727 90 X

Printed in Hong Kong by Aardvark Press

ALSO AVAILABLE
THE SECOND KIDSTUFF by Roger

KIDSTUFF
with Willie

By ROGER

ITV BOOKS
in association with
MICHAEL JOSEPH

Every day Gran feeds the slugs in her garden with a food called bait!

Now you've bought a new T.V. will we get better programmes?

Dad, if I grew from a seed was my picture on the packet?

You don't laugh much Dad, does it hurt to be old?

I can't be a footballer when I grow up 'cos my mum won't let me spit!

How am I to find the word when I can't even spell it?

If curlers are to make you beautiful for dad, why do you take them out before he gets home?

Mum, why do I keep on asking questions?

What a pity you have to get married before you can have such a lovely cake!

Mum if you were Queen would you be Lily the first?

Also please, should I put 'Amen' at the end of my thank you letter to my Sunday school teacher?

I know Mums make babies. What are the dads for?

Don't turn out the light! I wont be able to see my dreams!

christmas I got up so early, it was still late!

Well, if I cant have more pocket money, can I have the same amount more often?

Spiders dont wear knickers 'cos they have eight legs.

An Oyster is a fish built like a nut!

If I'd known you were going to be so bossy, I'd never have been born from you!

It must be Sunday because we're having dinner round the table instead of round the telly!

Before she cooked it, Mum fed the turkey lots of sage and onion and he ate every spoonfull!

Dad has wise eyes that can read anything!

Dear Aunt

Thankyou
very much for
the lovely
birthday present
Love JOAN x
x x

P.s. After reading please pass
the letter to another Aunt.

why do they
always collect
money on a
plate in church,
does the
vicar eat it?

Why do teachers get paid when we do all the work?

Grandpa's a blacksmith. he nails feet on horses!

When you get married, do you have to divorce your mother first?

Why didn't God make any straight rivers?

I like having the spots. I get more presents then!

Mum, Why am I always sticky?

Mum bought
a chicken
that had
swallowed
a plastic bag!

I'm not stupid!
I just have
a quick
forgettery!

Gran is old
on the outside
but young
on the inside!

I know whats best for me! I'm closer to me than you are!

IF beauty is skin deep, how deep is ugly?

I'm a boy at home and a mixed infant at school!

What do you mean, what's it called? It's called MINE!

After the cat scratched me, I ate her saucer of dinner while she watched.

Chips are made from potatoes because tomatoes are the wrong colour!

Lets be friends come to the toilet with me and I'll let you tear my paper!

How do pigs lay bacon?

Why won't you come and play Dad? I can't chase me by myself!

Dads lucky he's a builder, he plays on a climbing frame all day!

The man next door
killed his goose
at Christmas so
it wouldn't catch
cold!

Why is a
ducks
nose his
mouth?

I can't say how
happy I am.
but if I had
a tail I'd
wag it !

My dogs Just had puppies and I didn't even know she was married!

I don't like my new sister, she's got no hair, no teeth, and she won't talk to me!

Mum, now you have a fur coat, does that mean you're a star?

I don't like animal meat so mum gives me beefburgers instead!

Sorry Miss, but if you came from our house in the morning, you'd be late too!

I dont care if father Christmas comes or not, I'm fed up with being good!

If you didn't see me before I was born, how did you know it was me?

Dear Mummy,
I HATE YOU !
* * Love Andrew

Do Sausages grow or are they born?

thanks Mum!
that was the
best meal I
ever put in
my mouth!

Of course I'm
dirtier than my
brother! I'm
two years
older than he is

Mums weak
for cigarettes
but I'm only
weak for sweets!

I saw my first ballet today but I didn't hear one word because of all the music!

We went to the natural history museum, It's a kind of dead zoo!

Mum, who did all the cleaning and stuff before we got you?

How am I supposed to do up zippers, when they're at the back and I'm always at the front?

Why did the doctor keep knocking on my chest? There was nobody in but me!

The trouble with dying is it's for the rest of your life!

Sometimes you can see the lines where the planes scratch the sky!

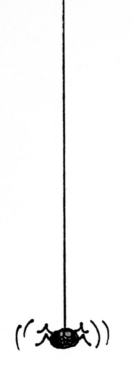
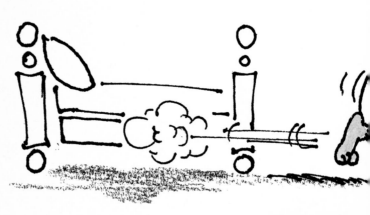